COMPLETE
SALVATION

COMPLETE
SALVATION

DEREK PRINCE

COMPLETE SALVATION

© 2001 Derek Prince Ministries—International
First published in the UK 2001, this edition published by
Derek Prince Ministries—UK 2007

This book was compiled from the extensive archive of
Derek Prince's materials and edited by the Derek Prince
Ministries editorial team.

ISBN: 978-1-901144-43-7
Product Code C83

Scripture quotations are taken from the New King James
Version (NKJV) © 1979, 1980, 1982, 1984 by Thomas Nelson,
Inc. Used by permission.

Editorial, design and production services by Summit
Publishing Ltd.
Printed in the United Kingdom by Creative Print and Design
(Wales), Ebbw Vale.

1 2 3 4 5 6 7 8 9 10 / 10 09 08 07

Derek Prince Ministries—UK
www.dpmuk.org

CONTENTS

INTRODUCTION

I want to emphasize that our salvation is *great* and it is *complete*, because I believe that many Christians who have experienced salvation have not experienced *all* that God included in the salvation He has provided. It is as if they are living in a corner of a little house, whereas they have actually entered a great big, wonderful mansion that God has prepared for them. In fact, I do not believe that there is a Christian on earth today who has experienced the completeness of all that God has provided in salvation—and I include myself. I thank God I am enjoying a lot more than I did when I was first saved in 1941, but I know there is much, much more for us all.

1

SO GREAT A SALVATION

In Hebrews 2:3, the writer asks: *"How shall we escape if we neglect so great a salvation . . . ?"*

It is a *great* salvation that God has provided for us through Jesus Christ. However, one of the great dangers is that we would "neglect" it— that is, not really enter into it. Neglect includes accepting our great salvation as just a theological fact or doctrine but not embracing it in fullness in our experience.

Understanding the Vastness of Our Salvation

In Ephesians 3:17-19, the apostle Paul prays for the people of God:

. . . That you, being rooted and grounded in

love, may be able to comprehend with all the saints what is the width and length and depth and height — to know the love of Christ which passes knowledge; that you may be filled with all the fullness of God.

I picture entering our great salvation as walking into a tremendous mansion. It has many corridors and different types of rooms. If we look, first of all, at the width — it stretches out as far as our eyes can see in either direction. Then if we look ahead at the length, we cannot see the end of it. Imagine standing on a grand staircase in the midst of that wonderful mansion. When you look down, you cannot see all that is beneath you. Finally, as you look up, it stretches beyond what you can take in with your eyes!

Paul's prayer tells us that God does not want us to remain isolated in some small corner of the mansion we have entered, but to comprehend — to take in and embrace — all the scope of our great salvation: its width, its length, its depth and its height.

Throughout the Bible, the word *salvation* has a very wide application. For many people it might simply mean having their sins forgiven and becoming "a pre-packaged soul for heaven". But there is a lot more to salvation than that.

Salvation is a biblical word for God's all-inclusive provision for man. It is used in the New Testament to describe all the benefits and blessings of God made available to us through Jesus Christ. It includes the forgiveness of sins, the gift of eternal life, the provision of physical healing, the power to live a life that is different— in fact, every provision for this life and the assurance of eternity in the presence of Almighty God.

The Importance of Trusting in God's Salvation

Psalm 78:12-54 describes the Lord's dealings with Israel in bringing them out of Egypt and then taking them through the wilderness. It also states why the Lord became angry with His people. Putting it into everyday language, God was angry because they had such a small view of Him and His salvation. Similarly, I believe that sometimes we grieve God by our small comprehension of the salvation He has given us.

If you analyze the passage, *salvation* is the all-inclusive word for every blessing and provision God gave them, from the time they sacrificed the Passover lamb and were delivered from Egypt until they entered their inheritance. It included protection from God's judgement through the blood of the lamb, the supernatural passing through the Red Sea, the presence of God coming down in the form of a cloud, being fed every day with manna from heaven, water gushing out of the rocks and so on.

However, despite all the *"marvellous things"* God did, the people sinned and rebelled in the wilderness, tested God in their hearts and spoke against Him. (Verses 17-20)

Verses 21 and 22 tell us:

Therefore, the LORD *heard this and was furious; so a fire was kindled against Jacob and anger also came up against Israel, because they did not believe in God and did not trust in His salvation.*

Have you ever considered what it took to feed some three million people every day? I saw a picture years ago of the freight train that would be required to carry the water and food for three million people for one day. It was a very long train indeed—and that was just for one day! God fed them in the wilderness for *forty years*. All that provision was included in their salvation.

Also included was the fact their shoes never wore out and their clothes never got old. When they were sick, God provided healing. In the heat of the day, He covered them with a cloud and, in the cold of night, He provided the warmth and light of a fire. God's total provision was summed up in this one word "salvation", used in verse 22 (in Hebrew it is *yeshuah*). Yet God was grieved because they did not comprehend the extent of His salvation.

Further on, in verse 41, it says: "*Yes, again and again they tempted God and limited the Holy One of Israel.*"

I confess that many times I have limited God in my concept of salvation. I have had a need and thought to myself, *Can I really trust God for that need?* I think most Christians today set limits to what they think God will do. These are not scriptural limits, they are just limits on how big we imagine God's salvation to be. We need to bear in mind that this grieves the Lord. When the Israelites set limits to what they thought God could do, it grieved Him. Therefore, let us resolve in our hearts that we will *not* set limits to what God can do, but rather believe in the all-inclusive, comprehensive salvation God has provided.

The Perfect Sacrifice of Jesus Christ

Hebrews 10:14 states what was accomplished by the death of Jesus Christ on the cross:

*For by one offering He has perfected forever
those who are being sanctified.*

His death was a sacrifice, foreordained by
God, on behalf of the whole human race.

When I taught English as a second language to
African students, one of the things that I
discovered was that I had to teach them the
significance of English tenses. A tense is the form of
the verb that shows the time of the action. In this
verse, two tenses are used and they are very
significant. The first is called the *perfect tense*. It
says, *"For by one offering He has perfected forever . . ."*

The writer to the Hebrews has just described
how the Old Testament priests stood ministering
daily, offering again and again the same
sacrifices, which could never take away sin.
However, speaking about Jesus, he says, *"But this
Man, after He had offered one sacrifice for sins forever,
sat down at the right hand of God."* (Verse 12) The
contrast is between the priests, who stood
continually and Jesus, who offered His one
sacrifice and sat down. Why did He sit down?
Because He was never going to have to make
another sacrifice! He had done it all, once and
forever. However, the Old Testament priests' job
was never finished, because their sacrifices could
not deal with the real problem of sin. Jesus' work
is complete. It never has to be added to, and

nothing can ever be taken away from it. It is forever. That is why the perfect tense is used.

Speaking about those who are appropriating the work of Jesus, the writer calls us *"those who are being sanctified."* (Verse 14) That is what we call a *continuing present tense*. Jesus' work was perfect, but our appropriation of it is a continuing *process*. We are being sanctified. And as we are *being* sanctified—as we are increasingly set apart to God, draw closer to God and appropriate more of God's provision and promises—we enter more and more into the full provision of the one sacrifice of Jesus Christ.

I was a philosopher before I was a preacher, and I observed that the Bible is the only book that diagnoses accurately the cause of human problems. The cause is stated in one word: *sin*. No other book diagnoses the nature and effects of sin or tells us the remedy except the Bible. If we had to deal with the problem in our own wisdom or strength it would defeat us.

Sin's remedy is a sacrifice. This is the message of the whole Bible, from beginning to end. Wherever there is sin, there *has to be* a sacrifice. All the Old Testament sacrifices were prefigurings (shadows or types) of the one, glorious, final, all-sufficient sacrifice which Jesus made on our behalf on the cross.

Before He died, Jesus' last triumphant cry

was, "It is finished!" In the Greek of the New Testament this is one word, *tetelestai*—the perfect tense of a verb that means "to do something perfectly". My interpretation is that Jesus' sacrifice was *perfectly perfect* and *completely complete*. However, our appropriation of the benefits of the sacrifice is *progressive*.

New Birth and Salvation

We need to make an important distinction between new birth and salvation. Let us look for a moment in John 1:11-13 about the new birth.

He [Jesus] came to His own [place or home] and His own [people] did not receive Him . . .

Thank God for the word "but" that follows. This was not the end! There are many wonderful occurrences of "but" in the Bible (see Romans 6:23, for example). In John's gospel, we continue:

But as many as received Him, to them He gave the right [I prefer to say "authority"] to become children of God, to those who believe in His name: who were born, not of blood, nor of the will of the flesh, nor of the will of man, but of God.

To be born of God is new birth. In street meetings, in the city of London in particular, I have had the privilege of leading hundreds of people into the new birth. I said to them, "If you want to be born again, there is one thing you have to do: You have to receive Him!" That is the key to the new birth—*receiving Jesus*. The text says, "*As many as received Him . . .*" You have got to open your heart personally and welcome the Lord in. He also says, "*Behold, I stand at the door and knock. If anyone hears My voice and opens the door, I will come in.*" (Revelation 3:20) What a blessing it is to assure people that if they invited Jesus in, He has kept His promise: He *has* come in.

The new birth is a one-time experience. A person never needs to be born again twice. Much of it is potential, in a certain sense: we receive authority to become children of God. However, authority is useless if not used. What we become depends on how much we use the authority that we are given.

When I ministered in Africa, I observed that an African's attitude is, "There is no harm in asking for it." If you give an African a pair of shoes, he will probably say, "Thank you! But where are the socks?" If he knows there is something to be received by asking, he will usually come and ask for it. Therefore, it is not difficult to get people to come forward in sub-Saharan Africa in an appeal. Rather, it is difficult to *stop* them! I struggled to teach my students that, once they had asked to receive Jesus, they did not have to keep asking. He *had* come in! The real victory was when they did not come forward again—because then they had grasped the fact that they had received Him.

In contrast to new birth, *salvation is an ongoing process*. It is not a one-time experience. You might be born again but, as for salvation, how far have you come? Salvation is referred to in three tenses: in the perfect tense, the simple past tense and the continuing present tense.

Ephesians 2:8 says: "*For by grace you have been saved through faith . . .*" That is the perfect tense. Translated literally, Paul is saying, "By grace you are having-been-saved." It is completed.

Titus 3:5 says: "*Not by works of righteousness which we have done, but according to His mercy, He* [God] *saved us.*" That is the simple past tense. For me, there was a specific moment in time when God saved me: it was about midnight on a Friday evening late in July 1941. There is one particular moment when we personally enter into the provision of God.

In 1 Corinthians 1:18 we find the continuing present tense: "*For the message of the cross is foolishness to those who are perishing, but to us who are being saved it is the power of God.*" The continuing present tense means "us who are continually being saved."

In summation, we have a one-time experience in which we can say, "God saved me." Through that experience, we enter into a salvation which is already complete: we are *having-been-saved*. But, at the same time, salvation continues to work in us: we are continually *being saved*.

A vivid illustration of this is Noah's ark. There are two main arks in the Old Testament: the big ark of Noah and the little ark of Moses. Both are pictures of Christ. The big ark speaks of *me in Christ*; the little ark speaks of *Christ in me*. Each of them speaks of Christ.

Focusing on the big ark of Noah, we see that salvation came through entering that ark. At a certain time, Noah and his family entered into the ark and *they were saved*. The ark was already complete and perfect. It had been built exactly according to God's instructions. It never had to be repaired; it never had to be adjusted or improved or recalled. It worked perfectly! And thank God it did, because it would have been too late if it had not! The moment they entered into the ark, they entered into a perfect salvation. But all the time they were in the ark, the ark was *continually saving them* from the waters that raged all around.

2

NEW TESTAMENT USAGE
OF "SALVATION"

I want to draw your attention to something that does not come out in any translation of the Bible that I know of. In the New Testament, there is one Greek word for "save". Putting it in English letters, it is *sozo*. This Greek word *sozo* is most often translated as "save" or "saved", but there are other passages where it is translated "healed", "made well", "made whole", "preserved", and so on. These other translations conceal the fact that salvation is being referred to.

To make this clear, I will give seven examples from the New Testament of the use of this word *sozo* where, if we did not have access to the Greek, we would have no way of knowing that the word being used is *sozo*—that is, salvation.

Matthew 14:36

> *And when the men of that place recognized*
> *[Jesus], they sent out into all that*
> *surrounding region, brought to Him all who*
> *were sick and begged Him that they might*
> *only touch the hem of His garment. And as*
> *many as touched it* **were made perfectly**
> **well**.   (verses 35-36)

This is part of the ministry of Jesus. What the
Greek actually says is they were "thoroughly
saved" or "completely healed". It is the Greek word
sozo, with the preposition *dia* in front, which means
"through" —implying *thoroughly*. Every person
was miraculously healed, or thoroughly saved.
In other words, healing was not an addition
to salvation, it was one part of salvation. It
is salvation applied to the physical body.

Luke 8:36

Luke 8:26-39 gives a record of the so-called
"Gadarene demoniac", a man who was totally
demonized. He would not wear any clothes; and he
lived among the tombs, cutting himself, shouting
out day and night. When Jesus came, the man did
one tremendously significant thing: he came and
fell down before Jesus and worshipped Him
(Mark 5:6). In my experience of helping people get

delivered from evil spirits, they have to be willing to submit to Jesus; otherwise they do not qualify. This man did absolutely all he could do; after that, the demons took over. But he had come to Jesus; and Jesus saw that, in his heart, was a desire for Himself. Jesus asked his name and the demons replied, "Legion", because many demons had entered him. Then the demons begged Jesus, "Do not send us into the abyss!" They pleaded to go into a nearby herd of swine instead and Jesus permitted it.

There have been a lot of interesting speculations as to why Jesus did this. My opinion is that it would have been agonizing for the man if the demons had gone out unwillingly. Therefore, Jesus gave them an option they were prepared to accept: to go into the swine. The swine then immediately ran down the steep slope into the lake and were drowned.

It is worth noting that one man could contain such demon power and keep it under control, yet the same demons could destroy a herd of two thousand pigs. That gives us some idea of the power of human personality. Many times in deliverance when I have heard someone's story, I have been overwhelmed by the fact that people could live with what they have had to fight inside them.

The people who kept the swine went and told about it in the city:

*Then they went out to see what had happened and came to Jesus and found the man from whom the demons had departed, sitting at the feet of Jesus, clothed and in his right mind. And they were afraid. They also who had seen it told them by what means he who had been demon-possessed **was healed.***

(verses 35-36)

The word used is *sozo* again. Thus, deliverance from demons was not an addition to salvation. It is a part of salvation.

Luke 8:48

Jesus returned to the other side of the Sea of Galilee and was thronged by a crowd when a woman with chronic bleeding came and touched Him. Jesus knew somebody had touched Him and asked, *"Who touched Me?"* She was afraid to admit it because, according to the Law of Moses, a woman with an issue of blood was ceremonially unclean and was not permitted to touch anybody. But she was so desperate that she went against the Law. When she realized Jesus knew what had happened, she came trembling, fell down before Him and confessed what she had done. In verse 48, Jesus said to her:

*Daughter, be of good cheer; your faith **has made** you **well**. Go in peace.*

Thus, deliverance from chronic bleeding is also a part of salvation.

Luke 8:50

Jesus had been on His way to pray for the daughter of Jairus, who was at death's door. The woman had delayed Him and Jairus' daughter had died. Some well-meaning, but negative, people sent a message to Jairus saying, "Don't trouble the Teacher. Your daughter is dead."

*But when Jesus heard it, He answered him, saying, "Do not be afraid; only believe and she **will be made well**."*

Guess what the word is? "She will be *saved*." What happened to her? She was brought back from death to life. This also is part of salvation.

Acts 4:9-12

After Peter and John had brought miraculous healing to the lame man who sat at the Beautiful Gate of the temple begging for alms, the religious leadership of the day had an inquiry. (I don't know whether you have noticed, but whenever Jesus healed people—and He usually did it on the Sabbath day—the religious leaders never bothered about the people who were healed. All they bothered about was their regulations for the Sabbath, which they claimed had not been observed. That is rather typical of religious people. They tend to get so absorbed with their little rules that they miss the really important things of God.) When Peter and John were arraigned by the Sanhedrin, Peter replied:

*If we this day are judged for a good deed done to a helpless man, by what means he **has been made well** . . .*

The word again is *sozo*. Thus, the restoration of strength and life to the body of a crippled man is also called salvation. Peter continued that it was through the name of Jesus of Nazareth that this had happened. (Verse 10) Then he said: *"There is no other name under heaven given among men by which we must **be saved**."* (Verse 12)

Sozo again. The healing of that man was salvation.

Acts 14:9

And in Lystra a certain man without

*strength in his feet was sitting, a cripple from his mother's womb, who had never walked. This man heard Paul speaking. Paul, observing him intently and seeing that he had faith **to be healed**, said with a loud voice, "Stand up straight on your feet!" And he leaped and walked.*   (verses 8-10)

Paul saw that he had faith to be healed — he had faith to be *saved*.

2 Timothy 4:18

This is a completely different use of the word. Paul, right at the end of his life, in jail and facing probable execution, said:

*And the Lord will deliver me from every evil work and **preserve** me for His heavenly kingdom. To Him be glory forever and ever. Amen!*

The word translated "preserve" is *sozo* again — save. Salvation includes the process of being kept by God for His eternal kingdom.

These examples are instances where the Greek word for "save" is applied to things other than the forgiveness of sins. They emphasize that salvation is *the all-inclusive benefit of the sacrifice of Jesus on the cross*. It covers every area of human personality and every need in any human life in time or eternity. Whether a need is spiritual, mental, emotional, physical, or financial, it is covered by the one sacrifice of Jesus.

I have spent years meditating on Jesus' work on the cross—ever since I was sick in a British military hospital in Egypt in 1943. God sent me a precious sister: a lady brigadier in the Salvation Army, aged about 76 and a real warrior of the Lord. She got permission for me to go out pray with her in a car. God spoke to me through another sister in that car, saying, "Consider the work of Calvary: a perfect work—perfect in every respect, perfect in every aspect." When I got out of the car I was just as sick as when I got in. But God had shown me where to find the answer: the work of Calvary. It was a perfect work, perfect in every respect. It does not matter what kind of need we have, the sacrifice of Jesus was perfect in every aspect. From whatever angle you view it, it was perfect.

Since that time (for nearly sixty years), I have been considering the work of Calvary. I never get to the end of it. And in the course of time I have discovered two ways of understanding and communicating the cross. There are two key words that I believe God has given me to explain what was accomplished by the death of Jesus.

The first word is *exchange;* the second is *identification.*

3

THE CROSS: EXCHANGE

The first way to view and understand the cross is contained in the word *exchange*. On the cross, a divinely ordained exchange took place in this sense: God visited upon Jesus all the evil that was due by justice to us, so that in return He might make available to us all the good that was due to the perfect, sinless, obedient Son of God. To examine the nature of the exchange, I will present eight aspects of it. A key chapter is Isaiah 53.

Jesus was punished that we might be forgiven

> *All we like sheep have gone astray; we have turned, every one, to his own way; and the* LORD *has laid on Him* [or made to meet together on Him, Jesus] *the iniquity of us all.* (Isaiah 53:6)

We have all turned to our own way. That is the problem of the human race, the one thing of which we are all guilty. We may not have robbed a bank, committed adultery, got drunk, or stolen; but there is one thing we have all done—turned to our own way. And God says our ways are not His ways. (Isaiah 55:8)

Going our own way is turning our back on God; and it is called "iniquity". It is a strong word in Hebrew, *avon*, which means not just doing wrong, but includes the penalties and judgement that follow doing wrong. The revelation Isaiah gives us is that God visited on Jesus the iniquity of us all. Thus, all the evil consequences of our wickedness came upon Jesus on the cross. He took the evil—all the judgement and punishment—so that, by a divine exchange, God might make the good due to Jesus available to us. There was no reason for it, except God's grace. God did not owe us anything. It was purely His measureless grace and His incomprehensible love.

Grace is what you can never earn. Some Christians do not really know what grace is, because they are always trying to earn it. But we cannot ever earn what Jesus made available to us through the cross. If we try to be good enough, we will never receive it. It is purely by grace. And it is received only through faith.

"For by grace you have been saved through faith." (Ephesians 2:8)

When I spend time meditating on what Jesus did on my behalf, my mind can never fully comprehend it. He came down, took our place— even *my* place—and endured all the inexpressible suffering that should have come upon me. It was grace.

Jesus was wounded that we might be healed

> *Surely He has borne our griefs* [or sicknesses, pains] *and carried our sorrows; yet we esteemed Him stricken, smitten by God and afflicted. But He was wounded for our transgressions, He was bruised for our iniquities; the chastisement* [or punishment] *for our peace was upon Him and by His stripes* [or wounds] *we are healed.*   (Isaiah 53:4-5)

First of all, Jesus was punished that we might be forgiven. Because He bore our punishment, God's justice is satisfied and we can have peace with God. *"Therefore, having been justified by faith, we have peace with God through our Lord Jesus Christ."* (Romans 5:1) Second, Jesus bore our sicknesses and pains and, by the wounds inflicted on His body, He procured physical healing for us.

(The word translated *griefs* is a word for *sicknesses*.)

Do you believe it? If you do, then one thing you have to do is say, "Thank You!" to God. Thanking is the purest expression of faith. (I believe that many times we miss out because we do not give thanks.)

Jesus was made sin with our sinfulness that we might be made righteous with His righteousness

> *Yet it pleased the LORD to bruise Him; He has put Him to grief. When you make His soul an offering for sin, He shall see His seed, He shall prolong His days and the pleasure of the LORD shall prosper in His hand.*
>
> (Isaiah 53:10)

On the cross, the soul of Jesus was made the sin offering for the world. According to the ceremonies of the Old Covenant, when an animal was brought as a sin offering, the man who brought the animal confessed his sin to the priest and the priest laid his hands on the head of the animal. The sin of man was thus symbolically transferred to the animal. Then the animal paid the penalty for the man's sin. The penalty of sin is death. Therefore, the animal was put to death as a substitute for the man.

The writer of Hebrews says, *"For it is not possible that the blood of bulls and goats could take away sins."* (Hebrews 10:4) The sacrifices merely prefigured what was to happen through the cross. When Jesus died on the cross, He was made the sin offering for the human race.

There is no way our minds can begin to comprehend what it meant for the Lord Jesus, in all His purity and holiness, to become identified with the sin of humanity and to be punished for us. I am not an outstandingly priggish person, but when I think of some of the sins that are being committed in our society today—the awful sexual abuses and abnormalities—I shudder to think what it would mean, even to me, to have my soul identified with those sins. Yet that is just a tiny, minute fraction of what happened to Jesus when He became the sin offering for us.

The writer of Hebrews also says, *"But in those sacrifices there is a reminder of sins every year."* (Hebrews 10:3) The sacrifices of the Old Testament never put away sin. They just reminded the people that they were sinners. Their sins would be covered for another year. But Jesus *"offered one sacrifice for sins forever"*. (Hebrews 10:12) He dealt with sin forever by the one sacrifice of Himself on the cross. And His sacrifice put away sin.

In 2 Corinthians 5:21, Paul was alluding to Isaiah 53: "*For He* [God] *made Him* [Jesus] *who knew no sin to be sin for us, that we might become the righteousness of God in Him.*"

Do you see the exchange? Jesus was made sin for us, that we might be made righteous. We are made righteous with *His* righteousness, not *our* righteousness. The best we can do is not good enough, because Isaiah also says, "*All our righteousnesses are like filthy rags.*" (Isaiah 64:6) However, one of my favourite verses says:

> *I will greatly rejoice in the* LORD, *my soul shall be joyful in my God; for He has clothed me with the garments of salvation, He has covered me with the robe of righteousness.*
>
> (Isaiah 61:10)

Not only are we given the garments of salvation, but we are wrapped around with the righteousness of the sinless Son of God. It does not matter from what angle the devil looks at us, he has nothing to say against us. We have been given the very righteousness of God in Christ.

Are you rejoicing that you are covered with the righteousness of Jesus?

Jesus died our death that we might receive His life

Going on with the exchange, Hebrews 2:9 tells us:

> *He* [Jesus]*, by the grace of God . . . taste*[d] *death for everyone.*

He tasted death in the place of every human being. As far as I understand it, the work of Jesus covered every descendant of Adam; but it did not cover angels. Jesus was the last Adam. (1 Corinthians 15:45) We can never comprehend why God should be so interested in Adam and his descendants.

God began the human race in an extraordinary way. Adam was created in a different way than any other creature. The Bible says, "*By the word of the* LORD *the heavens were made and all the host of them by the breath of His mouth.*" (Psalm 33:6) But when it came to creating Adam, God moulded a figure of clay. Then that divine Being—the second Person of the Godhead, the Word of God by whom all things were made that were made (John 1:3)— stooped and breathed into the man's nostrils of clay the breath of life. (Genesis 2:7) The Hebrew word for "breathed" is powerful; it is *naphach*. The *ph* sound is a plosive. God "exploded" breath into Adam! He imparted His life to him. Think of the physical consequences: a body of clay became a living human being with functioning eyes, ears and internal organs! The Spirit of God did it.

To believe in divine healing is very logical. If your watch goes wrong, you do not take it to the shoemaker but to the watchmaker. If your body goes wrong, it is reasonable to go to the body maker. And our body maker is the Lord, especially the Holy Spirit, because it was the Spirit of God that made Adam's body come alive.

When God came to redeem man—He stooped a lot lower. Jesus Christ stooped to the death of the cross. Then when He had risen again and appeared on resurrection Sunday evening, He re-enacted the creation of man in the new creation. It says Jesus *breathed into*, or upon, His disciples and said, "*Receive the Holy Spirit.*" (John 20:22) The word in Greek, *emphusao*, is the same that is used for a flute player breathing into the mouthpiece of his instrument. I do not envisage Jesus breathing collectively on all of them. Rather, I envisage Him going up to each of them individually and breathing into them the breath of *resurrection life*. It was His divine life that had conquered sin and death, conquered hell and the grave and conquered Satan. It was a totally victorious life. It was eternal life, divine life, incorruptible life, indestructible life.

This was the new birth. The disciples were born again by the Spirit of God and they passed out of Old Testament salvation—which merely looked forward—into New Testament salvation, which looks back to the accomplished historical fact of the cross and resurrection. To enter into New Testament salvation, you have to do two things: confess Jesus as Lord and believe that God raised Him from the dead. (Romans 10:9) This occasion was the fist time these disciples had believed. It was New Testament salvation! Jesus tasted death for us, that we might share His life.

Jesus was made a curse that we might enter into the blessing

Galatians 3:13-14 shows us probably the most neglected aspect of the exchange:

Christ has redeemed us from the curse of the law, having become a curse for us (for it is written, "Cursed is everyone who hangs on a tree"), that the blessing of Abraham might come upon the Gentiles in Christ Jesus, that we might receive the promise of the Spirit through faith.

What is the exchange? What was the bad thing? The curse. And what is the good thing? The blessing! Jesus became a curse for us, that we might receive the blessing.

I have often taught for one or two hours on this subject alone. It opens a whole new door of deliverance, healing and peace. If you want to picture a curse, consider Jesus on the cross. He was rejected by man, forsaken by God, under darkness, in agony, not on earth and not in heaven. He was totally rejected, totally unaccepted. That was the curse. But, thank God, Jesus was made a curse that we might enjoy the blessing of God.

Jesus endured our poverty that we might share His abundance

> *For you know the grace of our Lord Jesus Christ, that though He was rich, yet for your sakes He became poor, that you through His poverty might become rich.*
>
> (2 Corinthians 8:9)

Again, you do not have to be a theologian to see the exchange here. What was the bad thing? Poverty. And what is the good thing? I do not like to use the term "rich", because it has been abused by wrong teaching. I prefer to use the word *abundance,* because to have abundance means you have enough for yourself and more to give away to somebody else. (Second Corinthians 9:8 describes this as having *"an abundance for every good work."*) Jesus endured poverty that we might share His abundance.

Jesus bore our shame that we might share His glory

Think of Jesus hanging naked on the cross with people walking by and laughing at Him. It was shame. Hebrews 12:2 tells us:

Jesus . . . endured the cross, despising the shame . . .

So many people today are tormented by shame. But I have good news for you! Jesus endured your shame. He endured shame for all of us.

One main cause of shame, to be very frank, is that many children have experienced sexual abuse in their early years. But, praise God, there is an answer! Jesus endured shame that we all might share His glory.

Jesus endured our rejection that we might have His acceptance with the Father

On the cross, the Father rejected Jesus. Jesus cried out,

My God, My God, why have You forsaken Me? (Matthew 27:46)

There came no answer. It was the first time that the Son of God had ever prayed and got no answer. And He died shortly after of a broken heart. It says in Psalm 69:20, "*Reproach has broken my heart.*" I do not believe that Jesus died of the effects of crucifixion; He could have lived quite a while longer. Rather, He died of a broken heart—because of rejection. Why did He endure such rejection? So that we might have acceptance! God can now accept us as members of His family because of what Jesus endured on the cross. He accepts us and we become the very children of God.

I think at least 50 per cent of the people around us are struggling with rejection, because of the failure of parents, divorce, the general cruelty of human beings to one another and so on. But we can walk out into the world and say we have the answer. It is provided by the death of Jesus on the cross. Jesus endured rejection for us, that we might know His acceptance.

The salvation that we have entered into thus covers all our emotional needs. It is perfectly perfect; it is completely complete.

4

THE CROSS: IDENTIFICATION

We have looked at the word *exchange*. Now I want to consider the word *identification*. To identify with somebody means to make yourself one with them—to put yourself in that person's place. The cross involves a double identification, it is two-fold.

First of all, on the cross Jesus identified Himself with you and me as sinners. As the last Adam, He identified Himself with the whole Adamic race and He paid the penalty for our sins. He became our substitute and He died in our place.

However, salvation comes only when we respond with the other identification—when we identify ourselves with Jesus in His death, His burial, His being made alive, His resurrection and His enthronement. That is when we enter into what He has provided.

He has made the first identification; it is finished. But we appropriate salvation as we identify ourselves with everything that came to Him from His death onwards.

Jesus as the last Adam identified Himself with man

Two glorious titles are given to Jesus in 1 Corinthians 15. They are sometimes quoted inaccurately. Paul says:

*And so it is written, "The first man Adam became a living being." The **last Adam** became a life-giving spirit . . . The first man was of the earth, made of dust; the **second Man** is the Lord from heaven.*

(verses 45, 47, emphasis added)

The two titles are the "last Adam" and the "second Man". I have often heard people call Jesus the "second Adam" but that is not what He is called. He is called the "*last* Adam" and then He is called the "second Man".

On the cross, Jesus died as the *last Adam*— not last in time, but last in the sense that the judgement of the entire Adamic race came upon Him. Then, when He rose on the third day, He rose as the *second Man*—a new kind of man. He became the head of a "race" that had never existed before. He was the head of the body, the firstborn from the dead.

The believer's identification with Jesus

The apostle Peter says:

> *Blessed be the God and Father of our Lord Jesus Christ, who according to His abundant mercy has begotten us again to a living hope through the resurrection of Jesus Christ from the dead.*   (1 Peter 1:3)

Through the resurrection of Jesus Christ when we identify ourselves with Him, we are begotten again: born into the new creation. Since the resurrection of Jesus, God has done a new thing in the earth.

Now let us consider the implication of Jesus dying as the last Adam. Paul amplifies this in Romans 6. Verse 6 is in the middle of one of Paul's long sentences:

> . . . *Knowing this, that our old man was crucified with Him [Jesus], that the body of sin might be done away with, that we should no longer be slaves of sin.*

This is a very important statement. When

Jesus died on the cross, our old man (our rebellious, fallen, Adamic nature) was crucified in Him. It is a historical fact. We need to understand clearly that the old man is incorrigible. God does not try to improve him— He does not send him to church or teach him Scripture. He has only one solution for the old man inside us and the solution is *execution*. However, the message of mercy is that the execution took place two thousand years ago when Jesus died on the cross. Our old man was crucified *with Him*.

Paul goes on in verse 11 to tell us what to do: *"Likewise you also, reckon yourselves to be dead indeed to sin, but alive to God in Christ Jesus our Lord."*

What God did on the cross is a finished, historical fact. It is true whether or not we know it or believe it. But when we know it and believe it *and apply it*, it works in us. Just as Jesus was executed on the cross, so I believe my old, fallen, rebellious, corrupt nature was put to death. Death is the way out—the *only* way out—of the fallen, Adamic nature. And we take the way out through the death of Jesus on the cross— through identification. Paul tells us, *"Reckon yourselves to be dead indeed to sin."*

What does it mean to be dead to sin? I always illustrate this by an imaginary incident involving a bad man. By the standards of religious people, he was terrible: He drank whisky, he swore, he cursed his wife and children and he watched all sorts of bad programmes on television. However, his wife and children were believers. They used to sneak out on Sunday evenings to the local gospel service and he would always curse them as they left.

One night they sneaked out and had a glorious night at the gospel service. They came back still singing choruses and, as they walked into the house, they waited for the curse to come. But no curse came. Then they looked. The cigar was in the ashtray and smoke was curling up, but the man was not smoking. The whisky glass was there, but he was not drinking. Do you know what had happened? The man had had a heart attack and died. He was therefore *dead to sin!* Sin had no more attraction for him. It had no more power over him. He was dead to it now.

When Jesus died on the cross, our old corrupt, sinful nature died in Him. Thus sin has no more power over us; sin has no more attraction for us; sin produces no more reaction from us—*through identification*. I meet people who have travelled all around the world to get away from their problems; but their real problem goes with them, because it is the old man. You cannot escape from the old man by travelling. There is only one escape and it is by death—the death of the Lord Jesus on our behalf.

The second side of identification, then, is that we must identify ourselves with Jesus. And this we do *by faith*. We do it because the Bible says it is true. There are five basic steps in this identification.

We Died with Him

First of all, we died with Christ—past tense. It is an event that took place at a certain moment in time. In Colossians 3:3 Paul, writing to Christians, says:

For you died and your life is hidden with Christ in God.

They were still living on the earth, yet Paul said that they had died. When did they die? It was when Jesus died on the cross.

Then in 2 Timothy 2:11, Paul says: "*This is a faithful saying: For if we died with Him, we shall also live with Him.*"

His death was our death. But to enter into salvation, the sinner, through faith, has to complete the identification. We all have to say, "Yes, when Jesus died on the cross, I died too.

His death was *my* death. My old man died in Him when He died." Then we say, "Being dead with Him, I must follow Him: from death to burial and from burial into resurrection."

Buried with Him

Christ's death was followed by His burial. How are we identified with Him in burial? By *baptism in water*. That is why baptism is so important. The identification with His death is inward, but our identification with Him in burial is outward. It is a visible identification with the Lord.

Water baptism, as expounded by the apostles in the New Testament, is an act of open public identification with the Lord Jesus in His death, burial and resurrection. And there is not the faintest shadow of a doubt that in the early church every convert—every person who became a disciple—was immediately required to identify himself publicly by water baptism with the One whom he had confessed as Saviour and Lord. The way into the fellowship of the church was this way of baptism. In my opinion, this is the greatest privilege that can be offered to a sinner on this earth: to be publicly identified with the Lord. And it is not only before man but before the entire universe that this takes place.

In countries where there is a strongly anti-Christian government, water baptism is the decisive cut-off point—whether amongst Muslims, Communists, Jews, or others. You can say you believe in Jesus and they might get angry. But when you are baptized, all hell turns loose, because that is where you are escaping from their territory.

> *Therefore we were buried with Him through baptism into death, that just as Christ was raised from the dead by the glory of the Father, even so we also should walk in newness of life.*   (Romans 6:4)

Thus, every baptismal service is, in fact, a double service. It should be a burial followed by a resurrection!

In Colossians 2:12 Paul says the same thing:

> . . . *Buried with Him in baptism, in which you also were raised* [resurrected] *with Him through faith in the working of God, who raised Him from the dead.*

When we are buried with Him in baptism, then we have the right to follow Him in everything that followed His burial.

Made Alive, Resurrected and Enthroned with Him

There are three more stages, stated in Ephesians 2:4-6:

But God, who is rich in mercy, because of His great love with which He loved us, even when we were dead in trespasses, made us alive together with Christ (by grace you have been saved) and raised us up [resurrected us] *together and made us sit together in the heavenly places in Christ Jesus.*

Notice that the word *together* occurs three times. Jesus did not come out of the tomb dead. He was made alive before He came out of the tomb. Thus, we are made alive with Christ. Then we are resurrected with Christ. But we do not stop there. We are also made to sit together with Him in heavenly places. What is He sitting on in heaven today? A throne. Thus, we are also enthroned with Him!

We not only died, but were buried, made alive, resurrected and enthroned together with Christ.

All this is totally outside our power to achieve. That is obvious. There is no way we can work for it. There is no way we can be good

enough for it or deserve it. We can only receive it
by faith—solely by faith.

Many professing Christians have an uneasy
feeling they ought to be doing something to earn
salvation. The result is that they never really
receive or enjoy it. It is usually easier for the
worst sinners to get saved than churchgoers.
Have you noticed that?

God's Purpose

After Paul speaks about us being made alive,
resurrected and enthroned in Ephesians 2, he
reveals God's purpose. Why did God do it?

To demonstrate the riches of His grace

> . . . *That in the ages to come He might show
> the exceeding riches of His grace in His
> kindness toward us in Christ Jesus.*
>
> (Ephesians 2:7)

What a staggering thought! Not just in this
life, but forever and ever, we are to be the
demonstration of the riches of the God's grace—
for the whole universe! Whenever God wants to
show any created being the extent of His grace,
He will say, in effect, "Look at these people. See
how they're close to Me, worshipping Me? They

are My children! They were sinners, rebels, cast out, unprofitable, useless, enemies of Mine. Yet I've brought them near to Me for all eternity!" I hope you are prepared for that. I hope you realize that forever you are going to be the demonstration of God's grace.

Remember, grace cannot be earned. There are many things in the eternal counsels of God that we do not fully understand, but I think, in a certain sense, God had to let sin happen in order to have something to demonstrate His grace with. See? I am not saying God approved sin but, when sin entered, instead of saying, "It's all over," He said, "Here is the real opportunity for Me to show My grace to the whole universe." Up to that time He had shown many aspects of His character, but I do not think He had fully demonstrated His grace. So we are His "opportunity"! We are the people in whom God is going to show the whole universe the real nature of grace.

To make us His masterpiece

A little further on Paul says:

For we are His workmanship, created in Christ Jesus for good works, which God prepared beforehand that we should walk in them. (Ephesians 2:10)

Not only are we the demonstration of His grace, but Paul says we are His "workmanship". The Greek word is *poiema*, from which we get the English word *poem*. It suggests an artistic masterpiece. Thus, we are God's masterpiece, to show the universe the full extent of His creative genius! That's exciting, isn't it? And just to prove what He could do, do you know where God went for the material for His masterpiece? To the scrap heap! Do you realize that? God can do anything with anything. He created the stars, the sun, the seas, the trees and everything else; but to demonstrate His grace and what He could really create, God said, "I'm going to take these broken pieces of humanity and I'm going to mould them into My masterpiece." Jesus died to create a masterpiece out of the broken lives of men and women. What a message! What a revelation!

If you are not excited about salvation, I do not know how much of God's salvation you have really experienced. People say we are fanatical if we jump up and down and clap our hands. I was a logician before I became a Christian and I have to say that such excitement is the logical response to the revelation of Scripture. Just to sit and say, "That's good!" is inadequate and unrealistic.

5

HOW TO APPROPRIATE
WHAT GOD HAS DONE

I have described the provision God has made. It is perfectly perfect; it is completely complete. It remains for us to know how to appropriate it. I could end at this point, leaving a tantalizing vision of something glorious, but many of you would not know how to come into it. Therefore, I am going to describe steps by which we can appropriate what God has done. In my thinking, there are four: (1) to repent; (2) to believe; (3) to confess; and (4) to live out what we believe.

Repent

No one can ever bypass the first essential step, which is to repent. The whole Bible makes it clear that no one can ever be reconciled to God without repentance. I observe today that the church's teaching of repentance is very weak and ineffective; and the church suffers greatly as a result. Over the years I have counselled multitudes of Christians and my conclusion is that perhaps 50 per cent of their problems result from a lack of repentance. There is no way around repentance; it is important to emphasize this. Some people teach that repentance is negative and therefore we do not need it. It may be negative, but we certainly do need it!

In Mark 1:15, at the beginning of His public ministry, Jesus declared:

The time is fulfilled and the kingdom of God is at hand. Repent and believe in the gospel.

God never tells anybody in the New Testament to believe without first telling them to repent. In fact, you cannot really believe *unless* you have truly repented. You can go through all the outward motions and forms of believing, but the reality will not be there.

Repenting is not an emotion, it's a *decision*. The Greek word is translated "to change your mind" in secular Greek. Repenting is *changing your mind*: you have been living one way, but now you decide to live another way. You have been pleasing yourself, living by your own standards, doing your own thing; but you decide to submit to God and live *His* way; God is going to tell you what to do and you are going to obey. A person who has truly repented does not argue with God.

Some people want their problems solved in order to be able to do what they want. They have their plan for what they would like to do and be in life. But they are not willing to repent and submit to God's will. Repentance says, "Here I am, Lord. Do with me what *You* want. I lay aside my ambitions. You may have totally different plans for me, so I lay down my own desires and, God, I'm open to whatever You tell me to do!" That is repentance.

After the resurrection, Jesus explained to His disciples the Scriptures about His death and resurrection.

> *Thus it is written and thus it was necessary for the Christ to suffer and to rise from the dead the third day and that repentance and remission* [or forgiveness] *of sins should be preached in His name . . .*   (Luke 24:46)

What must be preached first? Not forgiveness, but repentance. We have no right to leave out repentance and offer people forgiveness.

I was once in a meeting in Southeast Asia where a minister preached an excellent message on healing. He pointed out how we can receive healing through the Word of God. The message blessed me, but at the end he said to the mixed multitude, "If you want this wonderful life and all these blessings, come forward and receive them!" He had not mentioned the word "repentance" once in the whole message. A lot of people came forward who were idol worshippers, but they did not get the healing they sought. The result was confusion.

Clearly, the people had not met the condition of repentance. But it was not their fault, because the condition had not been stated. We, with a background of biblical knowledge, can sometimes assume that people know they must repent. However, in many cultures people have no concept of what true repentance is. For some, repentance might mean inflicting suffering on themselves, for example. But repentance is *not* inflicting suffering on yourself. Jesus has endured all the suffering we deserved on our behalf. Repentance is making up your mind to change and be changed, letting go of everything you are holding on to and saying, "God, I'm at *Your* disposal."

On the Day of Pentecost, when the Holy Spirit had fallen, a multitude of people were convicted of their sins. They did not know what to do; so in Acts 2:37 they asked the apostles: *"Men and brethren, what shall we do?"* Peter gave them a three-step answer:

> *Repent and . . . be baptized . . . and you shall receive the gift of the Holy Spirit.*
> (Acts 2:38)

What was the first requirement? To repent. That is still the first step in God's answer. But it is not an installment deal; it is a *package* deal. We should do all these things at one time: repent, be baptized and receive the Holy Spirit.

In Acts 20, we find Paul speaking to the elders of the church at Ephesus, reminding them of his ministry.

> *. . . I kept back nothing that was helpful, but proclaimed it to you and taught you publicly and from house to house, testifying to Jews and also to Greeks, repentance toward God and faith toward our Lord Jesus Christ.*
> (Acts 20:20)

It did not matter whether they were Jews, Greeks, or who they were. The order was first, repentance toward God, then faith in Jesus Christ.

Believe and Confess

I do not know whether to put *confess* before *believe*, or *believe* before *confess*. In the New Testament, the two are not really separated. Let us see this in Romans 10:8-13, where Paul describes the conditions for New Testament salvation. I want you to notice the order. He talks about two things: the mouth and the heart. The first two times he puts the mouth before the heart; but the third time he puts the heart before the mouth. We do not tend to think this way but, in a certain sense, we get faith by saying something.

It is an interesting fact that where English says, "to learn by heart", Hebrew says, "to learn by mouth". Each is true. If you want a thing in your heart, keep saying it with your mouth! Conversely, if you have something in your heart, it will come out in what you say. Jesus said, *"For out of the abundance of the heart the mouth speaks."* (Matthew 12:34) Each is one part of the total process of believing and confessing. If you already believe something, the more you affirm it, the more you will believe it; and the more you believe it, the more you will affirm it. On the other hand, if you do not affirm what you believe, you will cease to believe it; and if you cease to believe it, you will soon cease to affirm it.

The word "confess" means literally "to say

the same as". Biblical confession is thus saying the same as God has said in His Word. It is making the words of your mouth agree with the Word of God. And it is essential in the process of salvation. You cannot really experience salvation without right confession. Look at what Paul says in Romans 10:8-9:

"The word is near you, in your mouth and in your heart" (that is, the word of faith which we preach): that if you confess with your mouth the Lord Jesus [or Jesus as Lord] and believe in your heart that God has raised Him from the dead, you will be saved.

What do we do first? Confess with our mouth. And we also believe in our heart. That is not the way we tend to think, but it is actually true to experience.

Then in verse 10, the third time Paul refers to the mouth and heart, he says, *"For with the heart one believes unto righteousness and with the mouth confession is made unto salvation."*

I grew up in Britain among people who were good churchgoers, some of whom were undoubtedly genuinely saved Christians. But no one ever told me what it was to be saved. For people in those days, religion was something "personal" that you did not talk about.

However, that is not the way it should be with the gospel. We *should* talk about it—believe and confess; confess and believe.

In the book of Hebrews, there are three passages that reveal the position of Jesus as High Priest in relationship to our confession.

> *Therefore, holy brethren, partakers of the heavenly calling, consider the Apostle and High Priest of our confession, Christ Jesus.*
>
> (Hebrews 3:1)

Jesus was the Apostle sent out by God to provide redemption. Having provided redemption, He returned to be our High Priest in the presence of God. But it says He is the *"High Priest of our confession"*. In a certain sense, if we close our lips on earth, we silence the lips of our Advocate in heaven. The more we confess, the more we release His high-priestly ministry on our behalf.

> *Seeing then that we have a great High Priest who has passed through the heavens, Jesus the Son of God, let us hold fast our confession.* (Hebrews 4:14)

Notice the statement that we are to *hold fast* our confession. That means we are to say it and keep on saying it, without backing off or getting discouraged.

Finally, in Hebrews 10:21-23, the writer returns to the same theme:

> . . . *Having a High Priest over the house of God, let us draw near . . . Let us hold fast the confession of our hope without wavering, for He who promised is faithful.*

This passage speaks not of the confession of our faith, but the confession of our *hope*. If we confess faith long enough, it becomes hope. *"Now faith is the substance of things hoped for"* (Hebrews 11:1); so when we have built a substance of faith, hope comes. (My definition of biblical hope is *a confident expectation of good*.)

In the first passage, we saw that Jesus is the High Priest of our confession. Then we learned that we are to *hold fast* our confession. Finally, we are told to hold it fast *without wavering*. What does *without wavering* imply? Let me explain with a simple illustration. If you are travelling in an airplane and the "Fasten seat belt" sign comes on, what does that tell you? Expect turbulence! What does *without wavering* tell us? Expect opposition! Here is where the battle is fought out, in maintaining our confession.

When it comes to making the right

confession, there is a dark, evil force that opposes us and wants us to keep our mouths shut. So we have to use our wills to open our mouths and say the right thing. Satan will use every kind of pressure, every kind of inducement to oppose us. He will use every kind of lie, whatever he can, with one aim—to get us to make the wrong confession. How can we defeat him? By maintaining the right confession!

Live Out Your Faith

Once you have repented and when you believe and are confessing, there is one more thing to do. You have to act out your faith. James 2:26 says: *"Faith without works is dead."*

Faith that is not expressed in appropriate actions is a dead faith. I want to suggest to you three appropriate actions that express our faith.

Be baptized

Baptism is your first opportunity to identify yourself openly with Jesus as your Saviour. Jesus said:

> *Go into all the world and preach the gospel to every creature. He who believes and is baptized will be saved; but he who does not believe will be condemned.*   (Mark16:15-16)

If you study the book of Acts, no one ever claimed salvation without being baptized. The early church attached urgent importance to it. I do not believe that we are entitled to claim *salvation* until we have been baptized. We might be born again, but I do not believe we have truly entered into salvation. We have no right to enter into resurrection life except by the way Jesus entered—the way of burial, the way of the tomb. It is clear.

When Philip led the eunuch to the Lord on the road to Gaza (Acts 8:26-39) and there was some water by the road, the eunuch said, *"What hinders me from being baptized?"* Note that the eunuch asks this, not Philip—so Philip had already made clear to him the necessity of baptism. Therefore, Philip went down into the water and baptized him.

In Philippi, when Paul and Silas were in jail (Acts 16:23-24), there was an earthquake and everybody was set free. When the jailer desired to be saved, what happened? He and his entire household were baptized the same night! They did not wait until morning. I have heard so many pastors say, "We have a baptismal service in three weeks. Put your name down." But that was not New Testament practice. Rather, it is, *"Repent and . . . be baptized."* (Acts 2:38)

I have seen some of the most exciting

meetings in my life when people have believed and immediately been baptized. One held years ago in a swimming pool stands out in my mind, when all sorts of people got baptized. There was a group of Baptists that came just to watch and there was such a presence of God that those dear Baptists said they wished they could have it this way! Just making baptism a ceremony in the church calendar is like making salvation something that happens if you come to church at Easter. It is detaching it from its real significance.

The first thing you should do when you have repented and believed the gospel is, thus, to be baptized. Find somebody to baptize you! I was teaching on this once in the university of Youth With a Mission and was very careful not to be controversial. I simply said, "Believe and be baptized!" I did not say anything about the method. Afterwards, people came up to me and said, "I want to be baptized now," so one of the professors there said, "This is your problem. You take them!" We marched off to the swimming pool and they got baptized the same hour of the night.

When the gospel is not exciting, I think we have lost something. When we do not have action like that, I think there is not much faith.

Give thanks

The second way to express our faith is by giving thanks. You can do this before being baptized, of course! The purest expression of faith is saying, "Thank You" to God. If you really believe what I have been teaching here, you will be thanking God even now. Otherwise you are either an unbeliever, a most ungrateful person, or are slow to believe.

Some of Jesus' miracles were achieved only by giving thanks. At the feeding of the five thousand (men) all Jesus did was say, "Thank You!" to His Father in heaven and five loaves and two fishes became enough for a crowd of perhaps ten thousand people. There is almost limitless power in giving thanks. Jonah was three days and three nights in the belly of the fish. He did not come out when he prayed, although he did a lot of praying. Rather, in Jonah 2:9, when he started to give thanks, the fish could hold him no longer. If you are "in the belly of a fish" today, start to give thanks!

Be led by the Holy Spirit

To conclude this list of actions, we need to take note of Romans 8:14, which says:

> *For as many as are led by the Spirit of God, these are sons of God.*

God does not have one single programme for every believer. The Holy Spirit will show you God's plan for your life. Do not pattern yourself on some other believer, because God has an individual plan just for you.

Simple but Not Easy

If you are saying to yourself, "There must be something wrong with me," because it sounds so easy yet it is not easy for you, my comment is this: Appropriating salvation is *simple but not easy*. Do you see the difference? Here are three reasons why it is not easy: we have three enemies that make it difficult.

The flesh or the carnal mind

For most Christians, the main battles that we fight are in our minds. Isn't that right? We have an enemy within us, which the Bible calls "the flesh". Those who live according to the flesh are carnally minded—they have an unrenewed mind.

> *The carnal mind is enmity against God; for it is not subject to the law of God, nor indeed can be. So then, those who are in the flesh cannot please God.*   (Romans 8:7-8)

This enemy resists the things that God wants us to do. We have to bring our minds into subjection to the will of God. Paul says in 2 Corinthians 10:3-5 that our weapons are mighty for *"bringing every thought into captivity to the obedience of Christ"*. Interestingly, the word for "bringing into captivity" refers not to a civil prisoner but to a prisoner of war. In other words, our thoughts are naturally at war with God, so we have to take them prisoner and forcibly bring them into subjection to God.

Satan

We also have an enemy without who resists us, called Satan.

> *Your adversary the devil walks about like a roaring lion, seeking whom he may devour. Resist him, steadfast in the faith . . .*
>
> (1 Peter 5:8-9)

The command to "Resist him" is in a continuing present tense. Doing it once with the devil is not sufficient. You have to keep on resisting him. He will keep on pressuring us, so we have to *keep on* resisting him. James tells us first to submit to God and then to resist the devil. (James 4:7) Then what will happen? He will flee! But Satan is stubborn. He has got to be convinced we really mean it. He probably will try four or five different tactics before he gives up.

The world

Finally, we live in a hostile environment, which the Bible calls "the world". Jesus told His disciples not to be surprised if the world hated them. He said, *"It hated Me before it hated you."* (John 15:18) Then, in verse 19 He used the phrase "the world" five times:

> *If you were of the world, the world would love its own. Yet because you are not of the world, but I chose you out of the world, therefore the world hates you.*

"The world" refers to people and systems that are not subject to the righteous government of God in the person of Jesus Christ. Therefore, anybody who is not willing to submit to God's righteous kingdom and government in the person of Jesus is in the category of the world. The world and the church should be completely distinct. The greatest problem for the church is when the world gets into the church. That is where our problems begin.

We thus have three forces that we come up against: the flesh, the devil and the world. That is why it is simple, but not easy.

Let us therefore press on, that we might learn to live increasingly in the fullness of the complete salvation that God has provided for us through Jesus Christ!

ABOUT THE AUTHOR

Derek Prince (1915-2003) was born in India of British parents. He was educated as a scholar of Greek and Latin at Eton College and Cambridge University, England, where he held a fellowship in ancient and modern philosophy at King's College. He also studied several modern languages, including Hebrew and Aramaic, at Cambridge University and the Hebrew University in Jerusalem.

While serving with the British Army in World War II, Derek began to study the Bible and experienced a life-changing encounter with Jesus Christ. Out of that encounter he formed two conclusions: first, that Jesus Christ is alive; and second, that the Bible is a true, relevant, up-to-date book. These conclusions altered the course of his life, which he then devoted to studying and teaching the Bible.

Derek's main gift of explaining the Bible and its teaching in a clear, simple way has helped build a foundation of faith in millions of lives. His non-denominational, non-sectarian approach makes his teaching relevant and helpful to people from all racial and religious backgrounds.

He is the author of more than 50 books and his teaching is featured on 500 audio and 160 video teaching cassettes, many of which have been translated and published in more than 80 languages. His daily radio broadcast, Derek Prince Legacy Radio, is translated into Arabic, Chinese (Amoy, Cantonese, Mandarin, Shanghaiese, Swatow), Croatian, German, Malagasy, Mongolian, Russian, Samoan, Spanish and Tongan.

Derek Prince Ministries is represented by 11 national offices and 37 outreach offices. The ministry continues to touch lives around the world.

Books Available from
Derek Prince Ministries

A complete list of Derek Prince's books, audio teachings
and video teachings is available at www.dpmuk.org

Derek Prince Ministries
Worldwide Offices

ASIA/ PACIFIC
DPM—South Pacific
PO Box 2029
Christchurch 8015, New Zealand
Tel: + 64 3 366 4443
Fax: + 64 3 366 1569
E-mail: secretary@dpm.co.nz

AUSTRALIA
DPM—Australia
1st Floor, 134 Pendle Way
Pendle Hill
New South Wales 2145, Australia
Tel: + 612 9688 4488
Fax: + 612 9688 4848
Email: enquiries@au.derekprince.com

CANADA
DPM—Canada
P.O. Box 8354
Halifax, Nova Scotia B3K 5M1, Canada
Tel: + 1 902 443 9577
Fax: + 1 902 443 6013
E-mail: dpmcanada@compuserve.com

FRANCE
DPM—France
Route d'Oupia, B.P. 31
34210 Olonzac, France
Tel: + 33 468 913872
Fax: + 33 468 913863
Email: info@dpmf.net

GERMANY
DPM—Germany
Schwarzauer Str. 56
D-83308 Trostberg, Germany
Tel: + 49 8621 64146
Fax: + 49 8621 64147
E-mail: IBL.de@t-online.de

NETHERLANDS
DPM—Netherlands
P.O. Box 349
1960 AH Heemskerk, The Netherlands
Tel: + 31 251 255 044
Fax: + 31 251 247 798
E-mail:info@nl.derekprince.com

SINGAPORE
Derek Prince Publications Pte. Ltd.
P.O. Box 2046
Robinson Road Post Office
Singapore 904046
Tel: + 65 6392 1812
Fax: + 65 6392 1823
Email: dpmchina@singnet.com.sg

SOUTH AFRICA
DPM—South Africa
P.O. Box 33367
Glenstantia 0010 Pretoria
South Africa
Tel: +27 12 348 9537
Fax: + 27 12 348 9538
E-mail: dpmsa@mweb.co.za

SWITZERLAND
DPM—Switzerland
Alpenblick 8
8934 Knonau
Switzerland
Tel: + 41(0) 44 768 25 06
E-mail: dpm-ch@ibl-dpm.net

UNITED KINGDOM
DPM—UK
Kingsfield
Hadrian Way
Baldock
Hertfordshire SG7 6AN
UK
Tel: + 44 (0) 1462 492100
Fax: + 44 (0) 1462 492102
Email: enquiries@dpmuk.org

USA
DPM—USA
PO Box 19501
Charlotte
NC 28219-9501
USA
Tel: + 1 704 357 3556
Fax: + 1 704 357 1413
E-mail: ContactUs@derekprince.org

If you have enjoyed reading this book and are interested in going deeper into the Word of God, then join our informal network of individuals, pastors and lay leaders interested in learning how to grow in their faith and respond to challenges of daily life.

To join and receive the following message FREE OF CHARGE, fill out this form and return it to our address.

You Must Decide

The decisive factor in human experience is not the emotion; it is the will.

Preferred format: ☐ CD   ☐ Tape   ☐ MP3* (Code: 4284)

* Please supply email address

Name _____

Address _____

_____ Postcode _____

Tel _____ Email _____

Role in the local church: ☐ Member   ☐ Lay Leader   ☐ Pastor   ☐ None

Age: ☐ 18–25   ☐ 26–35   ☐ 36–45   ☐ 46–55   ☐ 56–65   ☐ 65+

Marital Status: ☐ Single   ☐ Married   ☐ Widowed   ☐ Divorced

When it comes to learning, which medium is your favourite:

☐ Books   ☐ Tapes   ☐ CDs   ☐ MP3   ☐ Video   ☐ DVD

Number of Christian books you purchased in last year: ☐ 1–5   ☐ 5–10   ☐ 10+

Do you listen/watch: ☐ UCB   ☐ Premier   ☐ God TV   ☐ other _____

What Christian magazines do you read regularly? _____

What was the last great Christian book you read? _____

Derek Prince Ministries–UK
Kingsfield • Hadrian Way
Baldock • SG7 6AN • UK

Tel: +44 (0)1462 492100
Web: www.dpmuk.org
Email: enquiries@dpmuk.org
Reg Charity No. 327763

This is an introductory offer for those not already on our mailing list

C83RC